YOUR KNOWLEDGE HAS VALUE

Bibliographic information published by the German National Library:

The German National Library lists this publication in the National Bibliography; detailed bibliographic data are available on the Internet at http://dnb.dnb.de .

Imprint:

Copyright © 2019 GRIN Verlag
Print and binding: Books on Demand GmbH, Norderstedt Germany
ISBN: 9783346186355

This book at GRIN:

https://www.grin.com/document/591120

Yasin Sengöz

Supply Chain Design Seminar Work. Retailers, Relocation, Sustainability

GRIN Verlag

GRIN - Your knowledge has value

Since its foundation in 1998, GRIN has specialized in publishing academic texts by students, college teachers and other academics as e-book and printed book. The website www.grin.com is an ideal platform for presenting term papers, final papers, scientific essays, dissertations and specialist books.

Visit us on the internet:

http://www.grin.com/

http://www.facebook.com/grincom

http://www.twitter.com/grin_com

SEMINAR WORK – Yasin Sengöz

Name:	**Yasin Hüseyin Sengöz**
Course:	Supply chain design
Credit:	7.5 ECTS
Level:	Advanced (A1F)
Semester:	Spring 2019
Date:	2019-05-23 until 2019-05-31
Scope:	4 questions, 25 points per question, 100 points in total

Evaluation: Facts (10p) - Select facts carefully and write answers in your own words
(per question) Reflections (10p) – Do not stack facts only but reason, reflect and compare
Sources (5p) - Build your answers on multiple sources

Grade:
    U < 49p
    3 50-64p
    4 65-79p
    5 80-100p

Guidelines: Use the provided report template
Max 2 pages per question
Use Harvard reference system

Re-exam: Two revision rounds are offered (only to pass, not increase grade)

Round 1: Deadline 2019-06-05 at 18.00
Round 2: Deadline 2019-06-12 at 18.00

Question 1

In order to answer this question properly it is wisely to display pragmatic examples from the real-world and also include case studies which have been intensively handled and provide a steer clear overview of the various stages, different flows and operations which are involved throughout the supply chain of a t-shirt.

This question leads us to different approaches a company can undergo in order to fulfill market requirements and meet customer demand and also try to achieve a high customer satisfaction. (Schrauf and Berttram, 2016). An exemplary stage overview is shown in the figure A (Appendix-A), which is applicable for a t-shirt regarding the stages of a supply chain from (McColl and Moore, 2014). It is applicable for not only clothing; it is a generic description for the process a product goes through.

Typically, clothing brands and their markets are at a fast pace, in order to react quick in the supply change and meet the customer demand. The different strategies are mentioned in question 2. That is why the first process/stage Design & Administration is a crucial stage for this work environment. To give pragmatic examples, Zara and H&M (Ferdows et al., 2014; Perepu, 2008) try to design their products adapting to fashion trend and dedicated different teams to design clothing articles. In the process they are distributed worldwide, and IT-tools are used to make artificial virtual products which may appeal to the customers. The administration facilities, like Zara, are centralized (Ferdows et al., 2014) and aided with IT-tools. This makes sense since decision like purchase, close collaboration, idea creation (Lankhorst, 2009), problem solving, quality checks, internal administration are centralized which saves a huge amount of workload. If those activities would be decentralized the different facilities all over the world would need different third-parties and partnership in order to fulfill administrational tasks, if it is like Zara centralized, the company owns this competence in a bulked place, and can save cost and the teams are also able to collborate and make reasonable quick decision-making processes. The control and information is also in the hand of the company if a centralized unit controls the business activities. The retailing just has to focus on improving sales. When the products are shipped they are already "saleable", no set-up time is needed regarding pricing and decoration, the decoration is already given from the design layout retail team. In those micro- and macro business activities Zara, I think so, saves a lot of resources, can provide a quick time-to-market and has a high comptetitive advantage.

After the design & administration stage the production process starts. The design is given with the specific specifications and samples are made (Grönlund et al., 2010). Only if the given quality standard are met, mass production can start, testings are made before the mass production launchs (Bellgran and Säfsten, 2010). The production areas are mainly in asian countries like China, Turkey, India. These low-cost arreas are supplied by different suppliers with raw materials which are needed for production (Ferdows et al., 2014). So, the companies are moving or outsource the production process in order to have access on raw materials and the know-how of manufacturing clothes in those areas. Nevertheless, regarding to a sustainability and an awareness of exlpoting human labor this is not a good example. Zara has some facilities in Spain but mostly all of the cloth industry products come from Asia (Ferdows et al., 2014; Perepu, 2008).

The next step is the distribution of the produced products, in this case the t-shirt. It also depends how the strategical approach and the supply chain strategy are set up (question 2). Zara for example has big distribution centers in active high-traffic countries and continents (Ferdows et al., 2014), this will ensure them the flexibility to reach all the retail stores in a quick responsive manner to meet customer demands. The decision about the distribution system, like said before, is highly dependent on the company's overall and supply chain strategy (McColl & Moore, 2014). Though, in some way or another the t-shirt is distributed and delivered to the retail store. Zara even packages and labels the products before they are sent to store, to enable even faster and more expedient handling of the products in the shops (Ferdows, Machuca, & Lewis, 2014). This is also the last step, since the destination here is the retail shop. Now the customer is advertised or has a high brand awareness and recognition and loyalty (Hines and Bruce, 2007) to buy the product from the retail store. Nowadays e-Commerce shops are more convenient for the customer and this will, I think so, have a higher impact on the supply chain. May be companies still need huge hub-spots for their distribution centers, but I think the trend will come that a lot of small distribution centers and warehouses are needed in order to act agile in order to deliver fast and be responsible in changes throughout the supply chain. To meet the standard "same day delivery" companies definitely need smaller hub-spots for ensuring the distribution of the products.

Question 2

Supply chain strategy are based on reducing costs and improving the overall efficiency or they either focus on doing things additionally different as their competitors in order to meet a higher customer satisfaction (Hines and Bruce, 2007).

Not every supply chain strategy is suitable for each company and the market segments (branches) they are working in, it depends on the output, the goods, the service and utmost, the complexity of the handled goods and services (Ramanathan and Ramanathan, 2014). The table from appendix B, shows this in a steer clear overview.

The agile supply chain strategy is applicable for highly innovative product with more uncertain demand and supply (Hines and Bruce, 2007). This is reasonable, since the demand and supply of the served goods for the customer have a high level of uncertainty. Therefore, the supply chain shall be really flexible and adaptable in order to react to quick changes in the processes and demand/supply structure. This strategy is highly volatile and as explained needs to adapt itself regarding to market impacts and signals (Schrauf and Berttram, 2016). A pragmatic example is the Zara Case study. Zara delivers high fashioned, customer satisfying products in a short time-to-market and adapts its supply chain regarding the market actions and events (Ferdows et al., 2014).

Lean, which has his roots in the Japanese culture and also today all over in every production. The mindset behind lean is to minimize waste and contemporary improve the customer satisfaction and reduce cost. The value for the customer is always the gist of this philosophy (Bertagnolli, 2018). Lean concepts work well when demand is relatively stable, predictable and variety is very low. This leads to the implication that, the cost of producing and distribution the products will minimize. This strategy is most applicable to functional products with a lower uncertainty of demand and supply (Hines and Bruce, 2007).

The leagile supply chain strategy describes the hybrid solution of lean and agile concepts. The lean mindset and tools are used for predictable standard products and the agile principles used in comparison for the unpredictable products which have also long lead-times (Hines and Bruce, 2007). This combination also shows the beauty of the supply chains strategy decision. Companies have to find the most utmost suitable strategy and have to alter it in order to make it "work" in their work environment. For this, suppliers can be involved and even the customer to have a higher customer satisfaction, which shall the overall goal of all the activities in the company.

Risk hedging, the last strategy which will be mentioned here, is applicable for companies which produce less demand uncertain products chained with a high supply uncertainty in the supply process. Hines and Bruce (2007) describe it as follow: "Risk hedging is a trade-off strategy meant to gain without predominant loss and it is almost similar to lean strategy with more emphasis given towards supply uncertainty.". This means overall, to divide the risk of not receiving goods throughout the supply chain. In order to reduce the risk of not being delivered, for e.g., from the raw material supplier, companies try to select several suppliers which can deliver the same product. This will lead to a reduction of risk of finally receiving the ordered materials. This makes sense, since having only few suppliers can lead to a high dependency and a higher risk of not receiving ordered goods, nevertheless, if the ERP (enterprise-resource-planning) (ACIIDS, 2018) system is not automated enough or the suppliers are not involved properly in all the processes can lead to high administration costs, and a lower speed in time-to-market (Schrauf and Berttram, 2016). Since, time and resources have to be invested in order to select several suppliers which suit the demand and quality standards internally.

Question 3

For the begin it is wisely to start to define the terms outsourcing and offshoring since these are the terms which will be used frequently in this question section. Outsourcing is an abbreviation of "outside-resourcing" which means clearly to use external resources to perform tasks that were done formerly inhouse. In short, it means to give over tasks, which are not mostly the core competence of the company, to other companies and third-parties to entrust them with tasks on the obligation to perform them. The theoretical boundary of outsourcing starts from 0 and ends with 100%. Companies decide by themselves how much of control of the performed task they want to keep inhouse or give it to external companies (Szymczak et al., 2013). The purpose of outsourcing has different reasons, following some adequate reasons:

- Focus on core competence, in order to ensure competitive advantage (Szymczak et al., 2013). This is the utmost important reason, since companies spend many resources in research & development to ensure their knowledge and competitiveness in their core competence. If company no longer have the required core competence, or even neglect it, due to poorly designed priority setting companies can lose their competitiveness.
- Reduction of overall investment (Szymczak et al., 2013). As I said at the first point, they can mainly focus their resources in the core competence, and do not need to invest in different technologies/processes in order to be competitive in a special task and work environment.

4

- Greater possibilities to adapt to customer needs and customer satisfaction (Szymczak et al., 2013). Since third-parties are entrusted with tasks they have to deliver an adequate performance for the invested money spend on the supplier of the outsourced product/service. Mostly those companies are subject-matter-experts (SME) in the outsourced performing area and will ensure a high-quality work or service. If the customer demand is volatile, depending on the contract with the third-party, the partnership can be dissolved (Lexa, 2018), with this action the customer demand can be adapted easily. In comparison, if the investment was made inhouse in order to perform a specific task, the cost of the investment would be higher than outsourcing the task since the cost-drivers are not so easily degradable like the third-party partnerships (Cooper and Slagmulder, 2004; Ibusuki and Kaminski, 2007).

The difference between offshoring and outsourcing is that, offshoring is based on using country's resources to manufacture goods or provide services that were previously manufactured or provided in the implementing company's country of origin (McIvor, 2005). For example, having a third-party provided oil pumps in a high-quality standard is outsourcing, but if the oil pump production was transferred in another country (area with the highest value-adding) to the company's affiliate aboard, it is called offshoring. The purpose of offshoring, is describes briefly as followed:

- Reduction of operating costs (cheaper workforce; lower taxes; lower costs of leases, energy, transport; lower real estate and land prices; lower communication tariffs and cheaper means of production) (Szymczak et al., 2013). This is a really critical point since a lot of company's don´t know the difference between labor costs and labor rates (Pfeffer, 1998). Companies calculate with labor costs, and employees are getting paid depending mainly on their labor rate, which is in low development countries lower than in high developing countries like Germany or mainly in the EU. This leads to the confusion that the labor costs will be lower since the operational, administrational tasks will be performed by operators and resources which need lesser money investment and labor costs as high-development countries, (Pfeffer, 1998). But is it not always the case, the non-monetary aspect like time-to-market, speed, delivery, quality and customer satisfaction and long-term goals are not pursued with the most offshoring strategies from companies (Pfeffer, 1998). This is understandable, when the company tries to achieve short-term goals, but they should align themselves like the Toyota production system and adapt their whole mindset for long-term goals (Bertagnolli, 2018).

- Closeness of the target market (Szymczak et al., 2013). This is also often combined with joint-ventures in order to penetrate new markets. The affiliates already have experience in the country the company want to establish itself.

- Closeness to raw material resources (Szymczak et al., 2013). This is now an upcoming phenomenon for car manufacturers ensuring their partnerships with companies which have access to the raw materials for batteries which will be used for electromobility. They try to ensure the delivery and the exclusiveness of having access of resources which are drastically needed, with an progressive rising demand (Schneider et al., 2018).

- Ensuring high traffic nodes. This helps the companies like Zara or H&M in order to have a quick time-to-market metric and to be able to adapt their supply throughout these high traffic nodes (Ferdows et al., 2014; Perepu, 2008).

This showed, the factors of offshoring and outsourcing lead us to the conclusion that different factors influence the relocate decision of supply chains. The utmost critical point are costs. Companies try to be in low-cost environment areas in order to save investment costs, but nevertheless, the total cost of ownership is rarely taken into account in those factors and also the administration costs are not involved (Cooper and Slagmulder, 2004). This can lead to a fundamental wrong calculation.

Relocation can also be triggered by new high traffic nodes, when the company want to occupy these routes in order to have control and be able to supply their supply chain stages. Also the point to ensure new markets, or to penetrate new markets, companies like Zara and H&M (Ferdows et al., 2014; Perepu, 2008) penetrate new markets by locating new distribution centers to new markets. This makes sense, since the uncertainty is really high in new markets, and the companies have to adapt themselves regarding to the customer demand. And only by this decision to be close to the market, a quick time-to-market can be achieved.

A new upcoming point, in my eyes, is the fact that companies try to joint venture with companies in new markets and be able to have access to resource which are scarce and partial to acquire, especially in the electromobility sector. This leads to a change of supply chain locations and companies have to completely offshore departments or outsource tasks into new areas in order to compete and keep or even improve their competitive advantage.

Question 4

It is wisely to determine the term sustainability in advance before I proceed with answering the question. There are many literature resources which define this term, one, which I think is the most accurate is from Seuring and Müller (2008). Sustainability, and the attached sustainable development meets the needs of the current living generation of humans without the ability of future generations to meet their own needs (Seuring and Müller, 2008). This means that the current living generation shall develop a sustainable mindset and living culture to use the scarce resources existing on our planet efficient and with the background thinking of providing the same resources (or even better) to the upcoming generations. To connect it with supply chain design, management and strategy the overall goal is to minimize, or completely get rid of the ecological footprint caused the supply chain as a holistic construct (Johnsen et al., 2014). Personally, I think it is more than a responsibility every living human shall impersonate. It is our duty to make decisions, whether in every-day situations or work environment, positively regarding sustainability.

This written, we shall explain which risks can occur in supply chains. Sodhi and Chopra (2004) have a subtle description of problems and risks which can occur in a supply chain. They also categories the risks and give the drivers which can be seen in appendix C. Companies have to know which risks can appear while dealing and managing supply chains. As the appendix C demonstrates, there are different categories of risks (Chopra and Sodhi, 2004). Disruptions, delays, system risks, forecast, intellectual property, procurement, receivables, inventory and capacity. Chopra and Sodhi, sum quite a large scale of can-be risks in companies which manage supply chains. I would personally think the overview is enough to tackle the question. And we can also see that in a lot of departments and sectors within a company problems can occur, and individual problems are quite often connected with other risks (Lankhorst, 2009). This means solving properly only one risks doesn't mean solving the problem. Therefore, adequate problem-solving skills are needed to catch the root cause and handle precisely and understand the holistic approach/structure of the supply chain.

The following categories can be seen as "attached" to sustainability. Disruptions and delays risks. The following risk drivers are mentioned from Chopra and Sodhi (2004), and reflections are added.

Disruptions can occur when natural disasters occur in the world which affect the supply chain of the company. Since natural disasters can of course not be avoided completely and mother nature is acting with the law of physics, but the acceleration of the global warming can be slowed down, in order to delay eventual natural disasters or keep them in a range where they are not harming our locations of the supply chains. That means if we reduce our ecological footprint we can directly and indirectly help to avoid natural disasters by minimizing our ecological footprint (Johnsen et al., 2014). This improves, but only vaguely, the performance of the supply chain, since there are not so many breakdowns caused by natural interferences. It is also connected with the delay risk. This interconnection with delays can be made, since natural disasters cause delays or even complete shutdowns/breakdowns (Chopra and Sodhi, 2004) of supply chain, so no products can be distributed. Thus, the whole function of a supply chain is not given anymore and cannot handle the requested task to deliver the right product, for the right price, to the right product, to the right time with the right quality (Langhagen-Rohrbach, 2012). Delays can also occur when there is an excessive transportation material handling and when the transportation modes change. This carries different risk drivers, since the material is handled more in different locations and with different methods to transport. To be more sustainable the location decision shall include the current supply chain and the eventual upcoming rise of different location in the world, which means to locate the supply chain distribution centers in places where a huge amount of transportation material can be handled and the need for different, decentralized distribution centers will decrease. This can lead to lesser material handling, which can minimize the risk of border crossing problems, internal logistic processes, reducing maintaining costs for the facilities. Thus, the performance of the supply chain can be improved, since the centralizing of the location minimizes the risk drivers and the performance can be improved since the centralization in huge distribution centers allows the company a higher material flow with lesser material handling externally. Also, the change from different transportation modes, ship, air and land lead to higher risks and are time intensive. By changing the supply chain structure, of shipping different material dependent on their value companies can save money, like Dell (Chopra and Sodhi, 2004). Dell keeps a high-value inventory of components in the United States and flies them if needed to locations which are needed on demand, this is a high-cost approach and leaves a higher ecological footprint nevertheless they can decrease the air flights with the combination of using ship and land transportation for less expensive components. This mix of high and low value inventory and material handling can be adapted to the favor of the company and decrease the performance of the supply chain by giving adequate forecasts of the demand in different locations. This will save the company costs and also improves the sustainable aspect, since the optimization of time reduces high-polluting transportation modes.

Overall, by intelligent forecast systems (Rüßmann et al., 2015), different risks can be minimized and also the change of transportation modes regarding to the hub and sub spots of supply chain facilities in a way that high-pollution approaches are decreased (which are more cost-intensive than low-pollution transportation modes) companies still leave an ecological footprint but they decrease it, at least. This can also help to increase the performance, since the supply chain managers plan with lesser breakdowns, when they try to design the supply chain with a sustainable aspect. When companies increase the perception of the benefits designing the supply chain in a sustainability manner, it can lead to performant supply chain which secures the future of the next generation.

Nevertheless, forecast models need to be tested and approved with different resources, since this is not in the scope of the question a detailed description of the forecast model is not given.

Appendix

A – Stages supply chain

Figure A: Stages of supply chain. Self-illustrated, followed by McColl and Moore, 2014. McColl, J., Moore, C., 2014. Developing and testing a value chain for fashion retailers: activities for competitive success. J. Text. Inst. 105, 136–149. https://doi.org/10.1080/00405000.2013.829934.

B – Supply chain strategies

Strategies	Applicability
Agile	Highly innovative product with more uncertain demand and supply
Lean	Stable demand and functional products
Leagile	Products with unpredictable demand and long lead times
Risk-hedging	Functional products and evolving process

Table B : Product flow strategies, Source: Ramanathan, U., Ramanathan, R. (Eds.), 2014. Supply Chain Strategies, Issues and Models. Springer London, London, Page: 10.

C – Categories of risks and their drivers in a supply chain

Category of Risk	Drivers of Risk
Disruptions	■ Natural disaster ■ Labor dispute ■ Supplier bankruptcy ■ War and terrorism ■ Dependency on a single source of supply as well as the capacity and responsiveness of alternative suppliers
Delays	■ High capacity utilization at supply source ■ Inflexibility of supply source ■ Poor quality or yield at supply source ■ Excessive handling due to border crossings or to change in transportation modes
Systems	■ Information infrastructure breakdown ■ System integration or extensive systems networking ■ E-commerce
Forecast	■ Inaccurate forecasts due to long lead times, seasonality, product variety, short life cycles, small customer base ■ "Bullwhip effect" or information distortion due to sales promotions, incentives, lack of supply-chain visibility and exaggeration of demand in times of product shortage
Intellectual Property	■ Vertical integration of supply chain ■ Global outsourcing and markets
Procurement	■ Exchange rate risk ■ Percentage of a key component or raw material procured from a single source ■ Industrywide capacity utilization ■ Long-term versus short-term contracts
Receivables	■ Number of customers ■ Financial strength of customers
Inventory	■ Rate of product obsolescence ■ Inventory holding cost ■ Product value ■ Demand and supply uncertainty
Capacity	■ Cost of capacity ■ Capacity flexibility

Table C: Categories of risks and their drivers in supply chain, Source: Chopra, S., Sodhi, M.S., 2004. Managing risk to avoid supply-chain breakdown: by understanding the variety and interconnectedness of supply-chain risks, managers can tailor balanced, effective risk-reduction strategies for their companies. MIT Sloan Manag. Rev. 46, 53., p. 54.

Reference

ACIIDS, 2018. Intelligent information and database systems: 10th Asian Conference, ACIIDS 2018, Dong Hoi City, Vietnam, March 19-21, 2018: proceedings. Part 2: ..., Lecture notes in computer science Lecture notes in artificial intelligence. Springer, Cham.

Bellgran, M., Säfsten, K., 2010. Production Development. Springer London, London. https://doi.org/10.1007/978-1-84882-495-9

Bertagnolli, F., 2018. Lean Management. Springer Fachmedien Wiesbaden, Wiesbaden. https://doi.org/10.1007/978-3-658-13124-1

Bloching, B., Leutiger, P., Oltmanns, T., Rossbach, C., Schlick, T., Remane, G., Quick, P., Shafranyuk, O., n.d. Die digitale Transformation der Industrie 52.

Chopra, S., Sodhi, M.S., 2004. Managing risk to avoid supply-chain breakdown: by understanding the variety and interconnectedness of supply-chain risks, managers can tailor balanced, effective risk-reduction strategies for their companies. MIT Sloan Manag. Rev. 46, 53.

Cooper, R., Slagmulder, R., 2004. Achieving Full-Cycle Cost Management. MITSloan Manag. Rev. 44–52.

Ferdows, K., Machuca, J.A., Lewis, M.A., 2014. Zara, The world´s largerst fashion retailer.

Grönlund, J., Sjödin, D.R., Frishammar, J., 2010. Open Innovation and the Stage-Gate Process: A Revised Model for New Product Development. Calif. Manage. Rev. 52, 106–131. https://doi.org/10.1525/cmr.2010.52.3.106

Hines, T., Bruce, M. (Eds.), 2007. Fashion marketing: contemporary issues, 2nd ed. ed. Butterworth-Heinemann, Amsterdam ; Boston.

Ibusuki, U., Kaminski, P.C., 2007. Product development process with focus on value engineering and target-costing: A case study in an automotive company. Int. J. Prod. Econ. 105, 459–474. https://doi.org/10.1016/j.ijpe.2005.08.009

Johnsen, T.E., Howard, M., Miemczyk, J., 2014. Purchasing and supply chain management: a sustainability perspective, First Edition. ed. Routledge, New York.

Langhagen-Rohrbach, C., 2012. Moderne Logistik – Anforderungen an Standorte und Raumentwicklung. Raumforsch. Raumordn. 70, 217–227. https://doi.org/10.1007/s13147-012-0161-3

Lankhorst, M. (Ed.), 2009. Enterprise architecture at work: modelling, communication, and analysis, 2nd ed. ed, The enterprise engineering series. Springer, Dordrecht ; New York.

Lexa, C., 2018. Finanzierung für Start-ups: Die Vor- und Nachteile von Venture Capital. BASIC Think. URL https://www.basicthinking.de/blog/2018/03/22/venture-capital-finanzierung/ (accessed 7.25.18).

McColl, J., Moore, C., 2014. Developing and testing a value chain for fashion retailers: activities for competitive success. J. Text. Inst. 105, 136–149. https://doi.org/10.1080/00405000.2013.829934

McIvor, R., 2005. The outsourcing process: strategies for evaluation and management. Cambridge University Press, Cambridge; New York.

Perepu, I., 2008. H&M´s Supply Chain Management Practices, ICMR Center for Management Research.

Ramanathan, U., Ramanathan, R. (Eds.), 2014. Supply Chain Strategies, Issues and Models. Springer London, London. https://doi.org/10.1007/978-1-4471-5352-8

Rüßmann, M., Lorenz, M., Gerbert, P., Waldner, M., Justus, J., Engel, P., Harnisch, M., 2015. Industry 4.0: The Future of Productivity and Growth in Manufacturing 20.

Schneider, G., Goll, D., Bernthaler, T., Kopp, A., Rieger, T., Schubert, T., Schuller, D., 2018. Pulvertechnisch hergestellte Werkstoffe für die Elektromobilität — Teil 1: Batterien. Keram. Z. 70, 44–49. https://doi.org/10.1007/s42410-018-0031-x

Schrauf, S., Berttram, P., 2016. Industry 4.0: How digitization makes the supply chain more efficient, agile, and customer-focused. Strategy & Supply chain 4.0 – the next generation digital supply chain. McKinsey&Company.

Seuring, S., Müller, M., 2008. From a literature review to a conceptual framework for sustainable supply chain management. J. Clean. Prod. 16, 1699–1710. https://doi.org/10.1016/j.jclepro.2008.04.020

Szymczak, M., Szuster, M., Wieteska, G., Baraniecka, A., 2013. Supply Chain Management, in: Szymczak, M. (Ed.), Managing Towards Supply Chain Maturity. Palgrave Macmillan UK, London, pp. 9–44. https://doi.org/10.1057/9781137359667_2